101 ANSWE
MONEY PROBLEMS

50 FACTS ABOUT INDEBTEDNESS
30 REASONS FOR LACK
21 STEPS TO OVERCOME LACK

@ 2000 Matthew Ashimolowo
Published by Mattyson Media an imprint of MAMM
Matthew Ashimolowo Media Ministries
57 Waterden Road
Hackney Wick
London
E15 2EE

Bible quotes are from the King James Bible
unless otherwise stated.
ISBN 1 874 646-31-7

50 FACTS ABOUT INDEBTEDNESS

Many people spend twenty percent of their income servicing their debt.

Many are bound by compulsive buying.

We waste money everytime we see some cheap things and buy them.

Credit cards in the hand of a compulsive buyer leads to poverty.

Going into debt is an indirect training for your children to follow the same.

Borrowing is the father of bankruptcy.

Indebtedness is an evil spirit which has your destruction as its ultimate goal.

Debtors are presumptuous that they will have a job tomorrow.

Debt makes Christians to forget that they are promise keepers.

Thirty percent of home equity is to pay out debt.

Remember that only eight out of twelve months income belongs to you.

Indebtedness spreads faster than any disease.

Indebtedness makes you groan when you want to give God ten percent after the thirty two percent has gone to the government in income tax and national insurance contributions.

Unpaid bills stay on your mind like a bad dream.

Debt makes you and your wife to struggle despite your wages.

Debt drains the joy out of pay day.

Indebtedness causes so many family problems and tensions.

Debt tempts you to ignore the tithe.

Lies and deception are easier for debtors than those who are debt free.

Indebtedness may cause the courts to determine what you spend your money on.

Debtors become enslaved to the system of the world.

The 'buy now pay later' marketing strategy enslaves you and your children.

Many Christian children have been born in the atmosphere of debt. When you bring your children up as debtors, you have clearly disobeyed the Lord.

"Train up a child in the way he should go: and when he is old, he will not depart from it."   Proverbs 22: 6

Borrowing is the guaranteed passport to financial slavery.

"The rich ruleth over the poor, and the borrower is servant to the lender" Proverbs 22: 7

Unless there is a change, generation upon generation will be held in financial bondage.

To the debtor, burdens are added, woes are multiplied, peace is subtracted, and the mind is divided.

The presence of debt is the doorway to worry.

Debt is the reason for a lot of sleepless nights.

Unsettled debt makes people to question your integrity.

Responsible people feel the grind of borrowing inside their being.

Indebtedness can lead to family acrimony.

Indebtedness is the root of many divorce cases.

Remember indebtedness brings you under a curse.

Debt invites the spirit of fear into your home.

Several men have lost their confidence through Indebtedness.

A family in debt is a family in stress.

Debt between friends is one of the causes of their separation.

The spirit of debt is a bad master, it rules and ruins.

Indebtedness can frustrate the vision of a church.

Debt can cause arrested development.

Drugs and alcohol dependency often come out of indebtedness.

Indebtedness have often led to behaviours that lead to a sack.

All your financial decisions as a borrower could be subject to the approval of the courts, or the lender.

The lender determines your movement.

"The rich ruleth over the poor, and the borrower is servant to the lender."
Proverbs 22:7

Debt forces you to reject the leading of the Holy Spirit to give to God.

Indebtedness renders someone useless for the promotion of the Kingdom of God.

If you cannot imagine Jesus in debt, then it is not the lifestyle for you.

Debt is a thief that robs one of time.

Debt transfers your wealth to the already wealthy.

Debt makes you presume and forecast the future. If you presume on the current value of your property and borrow, you may not be able to pay it back.

30 REASONS FOR LACK

Ignorance of the biblical covenant of prosperity.

Belief that there is a conspiracy to keep you poor.

Belief that currency is something hard to earn.

Developing "fruit eater" mentality and not that of a "seed sower".

Believing that a good job is the source of creating prosperity.

Saving but not saving smartly.

Living beyond one's means.

Irresponsible use of resources.

Trying to get rich quick.

Withholding benevolence.

Cheating.

" *A false balance is an abomination to the Lord: but a just weight is his delight*"
Proverbs 11:1

Refusing to try again because of previous failure.

Downward investment instead of upward investment (spending money on things which depreciate).

Measuring your life by material things only.

Making your financial well-being dependent on someone else.

Latent belief that only greedy people can be blessed.

I don't have the capital it takes to start off.

Mythical Statements:

I was not born under a lucky star.

It is not what you know but whom you know.

I was not born with a silver spoon

in my mouth.

Refusing to take risks and investing.

Bad teaching in the church:

Prosperity is of the devil.

(What will be, will be).

Generational curse of poverty.

"Christ has redeemed us from the curse of the law, being made a curse for us: for it is written, Cursed is every one that hangeth on a tree: That the blessing of the Gentiles through Jesus Christ; that we might receive the promise of the Spirit through faith."
Galatians 3:13-14

The lack of godly purpose.

Foolishness - a fool and his money are soon parted.

Get rich quick schemes.

Bingo
Gambling
Lottery

The belief that big brother, the government owes you.

Lack of time to serve the Lord.

"Thus speaketh the Lord hosts, saying, This people say, The time is not come, the time that the LORD'S house should be built."
Haggai 1:2

Unwillingness to build the Kingdom of God.

Neglect for the things of the Lord.

"Is it time for you, O ye, to dwell in your cieled houses, and this house lie wasted"
Haggai 1: 4

Preferring personal comfort to the progress of God's Work.

"Is it time for you, O ye, to dwell in your cieled houses, and this house lie wasted"
Haggai 1: 4

Withholding the tithe and the offering.

"Ye are cursed with a curse: for ye have robbed me, even this whole nation. Bring ye all the tithes into the storehouse, that there may be meat in mine house, and prove me now herewith, saith the LORD of hosts, if I will not open the windows, and pour you out a blessing, that there shall not be room enough to receive it"   *Malachi 3: 9 - 10*

21 STEPS TO OVERCOME LACK

OVERCOME LACK

Replace false belief.

"For as he thinketh in his heart, so is he: Eat and drink, saith he to thee; but his heart is not with thee" Proverbs 23:7

Have a clear vision for life.

"And the Lord answered me, and said, Write the vision, and make it plain upon tables, that he may run that readeth it. For the vision is yet for an appointed time, but at the end it shall speak, and not lie: though it tarry, wait for it; because it will surely come, it will not tarry."   Habakkuk 2:2-3

Run with the Vision.

For the vision is yet for an appointed time, but at the end it shall speak, and not lie: though it tarry, wait for it; because it will surely come, it will not tarry."
Habakkuk 2:3

There is a job, business, vocation near you. It is locked up, waiting for you.

"For where your treasure is, there will your heart be also" Matthew 6: 21

Make yourself a lifetime student of the Word.

"Study to shew thyself approved unto God, a workman that needeth not to be ashamed, rightly dividing the word of truth."   2 Timothy 2:15

Save a portion of all you earn. Spend less save more.

"A good man leaveth an inheritance to his children's children: and the wealth of the sin is laid up for the just." Proverbs 13:22

Do not spend what you do not have. It is like reaping where you did not sow.

Remember what belongs to God.
Tithe

"Bring ye all the tithes into the storehouse, that there be meat in mine house, and prove me now herewith, saith the LORD of hosts, if I will not open the windows of heaven, and pour you out a blessing, that there shall not be room enough to receive it." Malachi 3:10

Offerings

"Every man shall give as he is able, according to the blessing of the LORD thy God which he hath given thee." Deuteronomy 16:17

Vows

"Vow, and pay unto the LORD your God: let all that be round about him bring presents unto him that ought to be feared." Psalms 76:11

Live below expectation.

"Let your conversation be without covetousness; and be content with such things as ye have: for he that said, I will never leave thee, nor forsake thee." Hebrews 13:5

Check out various investment opportunities.

Hard Assets
Liquid Money
Bonds and Shares

Repentance of bad attitude to giving and using God's provision.

"Thus saith the LORD of hosts; Consider your ways." Haggai 1:7

God requires reverence.

"Then Zerubbabel the son of Shealtiel, and Joshua the son of Josedech, the high priest, with all the remnant of the people, obeyed the voice of the LORD their God, and the words of Haggai the prophet, as the Lord their God had sent him, and the people did fear before the LORD."   Haggai 1: 12

Learn to receive God's instruction and what He says.

"A wise man will hear, and increase learning, and a man of understanding shall attain unto wise counsels." Proverbs 1:5

Recognise the deposit of God in your life.

"Now unto him that is able to do exceeding abundantly above all that we ask or think, according to the power that worketh in us." Ephesians 3:20

Be moved by God's Word, not circumstances.

"Heaven and earth shall pass away; but my words shall not pass away." Luke 21:33

Learn from others.

"And the things that thou hast heard of me among many witnesses, the same commit thou to faithful men, who shall be able to teach others also." 2 Timothy 2:2

Use the keys of the Kingdom.

"And I will give unto thee the keys of the kingdom of heaven: and whatsoever thou shalt bind on earth shall be bound in heaven; and whatsover thou shalt loose on earth shall be loosed in heaven." Matthew 16:17

Know what you want and why.

".....What will ye that I shall do unto you?"   Matthew 20:32b

Exercise the anointing to get wealth.

""But thou shalt remember the LORD thy God: for it is he that giveth thee power to get wealth, that he may establish his covenant which he sware unto thy fathers, as it is this day." *Deuteronomy 8:18*

Plan, Plan, Plan.

"A house is built by wisdom and becomes strong through good sense. Through knowledge its rooms are filled with all sorts of precious riches and valuables."
Proverbs 24:3-4   New Living Translation

Become a Kingdom Promoter.

NOTES

The twenty five percent income indicated on page 17 is for low band income earners in the United Kingdom, other rates may apply else where.

The seven percent National Insurance contribution is also only as it applies in the United Kingdom, other rates may apply elsewhere.

SCRIPTURES ON FINANCE AND PROSPERITY

"Through wisdom is an house builded; and by understanding it is established: And by knowledge shall the chambers be filled with all precious and pleasant riches. A wise man is strong; yea, a man of knowledge increaseth strength. For by wise counsel thou shalt make thy war: and in multitude of counsellors there is safety.
Proverbs 24:3-6

"Give, and it shall be given unto you; good measure, pressed down, and shaken together, and running over, shall men give into your bosom. For with the same measure that ye mete withal it shall be measured to you again." Luke 6:38

"The thoughts of the diligent tend only to plenteousness; but of every one that is hasty only to want." Proverbs 21:5

"By humility and the fear of the LORD are riches, and honor, and life." Proverbs 22:4

"Cast thy bread upon the waters: for thou shalt find it after many days." Ecclesiastes 11:1

"He that oppresseth the poor to increase his riches, and he that giveth to the rich, shall surely come to want." Proverbs 22:16

"Poverty and shame shall be to him that refuseth instruction: but he that regardeth reproof shall be honored." Proverbs 13:18

*"He that covereth his sins shall not prosper: but whoso confesseth
and forsaketh them shall have mercy."*   Proverbs 28:13

*"There is that scattereth, and yet increaseth; and there is that withholdeth more than is
meet, but it tendeth to poverty. The liberal soul shall be made fat: and he that
watereth shall be watered also himself. He that withholdeth corn, the people shall curse
him: but blessing shall be upon the head of him that selleth it."*
Proverbs 11:24-26

*"The rich ruleth over the poor, and the borrower is servant to the
lender."*   Proverbs 22:7

"And Abram was very rich in cattle, in silver, and in gold.!"
Genesis 13:2

"Moreover, brethren, we do you to wit of the grace of God bestowed on the churches of Macedonia; How that in a great trial of affliction the abundance of their joy and their deep poverty abounded unto the riches of their liberality. For to their power, I bear record, yea, and beyond their power they were willing of themselves; Praying us with much intreaty that we would receive the gift, and take upon us the fellowship of the ministering to the saints. And this they did, not as we hoped, but first gave their own selves to the Lord, and unto us by the will of God. Insomuch that we desired Titus, that as he had begun, so he would also finish in you the same grace also. Therefore, as ye abound in every thing, in faith, and utterance, and knowledge, and in all diligence, and in your love to us, see that ye abound in this grace also. I speak not by commandment, but by occasion of the forwardness of others, and to prove the sincerity of your love. For ye know the grace of our Lord Jesus Christ, that, though he was rich, yet for your sakes he became poor, that ye through his poverty might be rich. And herein I give my advice: for this is expedient for you, who have begun before, not only to do, but also to be forward a year ago. 1 Corinthians 8:1-10

Now therefore perform the doing of it; that as there was a readiness to will, so there may be a performance also out of that which ye have. For if there be first a willing mind, it is accepted according to that a man hath, and not according to that he hath not."   2 Corinthians 8:11-12

"For as the rain cometh down, and the snow from heaven, and returneth not thither, but watereth the earth, and maketh it bring forth and bud, that it may give seed to the sower, and bread to theeater: So shall my word be that goeth forth out of my mouth: it shall not return unto me void; but it shall accomplish that which I please, and it shall prosper in the thing whereto I sent it. For ye shall go out with joy, and be led forth with peace: the mountains and the hills shall break forth before you into singing, and all the trees of the field shall clap their hands. Instead of the thorn shall come up the fir tree, and instead of the brier shall come up the myrtle tree: and it shall be to the LORD for a name, for an everlasting sign that shall not be cut off."
Isaiah 55:10-13

"Honor the LORD with thy substance, and with the firstfruits of all thine increase: So shall thy barns be filled with plenty, and thy presses shall burst out with new wine."   Proverbs 3:9,10

"He that giveth unto the poor shall not lack: but he that hideth his eyes shall have many a curse."   Proverbs 28:27

"He that hath a bountiful eye shall be blessed; for he giveth of his bread to the poor."   Proverbs 22:9

"If ye walk in my statutes, and keep my commandments, and do them; Then I will give you rain in due season, and the land shall yield her increase, and the trees of the field shall yield their fruit. For I will have respect unto you, and make you fruitful, and multiply you, and establish my covenant with you. And ye shall eat old store, and bring forth the old because of the new."
Leviticus 26:3-4, 9-10

*"In that night did God appear unto Solomon, and said unto him,
"Ask what I shall give thee. And Solomon said unto God, Thou hast shewed great mercy
unto David my father, and hast made me to reign in his stead. Now, O LORD God, let thy
promise unto David my father be established: for thou hast made me king over a
people like the dust of the earth in multitude. Give me now wisdom and knowledge, that I
may go out and come in before this people: for who can judge this thy people, that is so
great?
And God said to Solomon, Because this was in thine heart, and thou hast not asked riches,
wealth, or honor, nor the life of thine enemies, neither yet hast asked long life; but hast
asked wisdom and knowledge for thyself, that thou mayest judge my people, over whom I
have made thee king: Wisdom and knowledge is granted unto thee; and I will give thee
riches, and wealth, and honor, such as none of the kings have had that have been before
thee, neither shall there any after thee have the like."*
2 Chronicles 1:7-12

"Bring ye all the tithes into the storehouse, that there may be meat in mine house, and prove me now herewith, saith the LORD of hosts, if I will not open you the windows of heaven, and pour you out a blessing, that there shall not be room enough to eceive it. And I will rebuke the devourer for your sakes, and he shall not destroy the fruits of your ground; neither shall your vine cast herfruit before the time in the field, saith the LORD of hosts. And all nations shall call you blessed: for ye shall be a delightsome land, saith the LORD of hosts."
Malachi 3:10-12

"But my God shall supply all your need according to his riches in glory by Christ Jesus." Philippians 4:19

"And he sought God in the days of Zechariah, who had understanding in the visions of God: and as long as he sought the LORD, God made him to prosper." 2 Chronicles 26:5

"Beloved, I wish above all things that thou mayest prosper and be in health, even as thy soul prospereth. For I rejoiced greatly, when the brethren came and testified of the truth that is in thee, even as thou walkest in the truth. I have no greater joy than to hear that my children walk in truth."
3 John 2-4

"The thoughts of the diligent tend only to plenteousness; but of every one that is hasty only to want." Proverbs 21:5

"A good man leaveth an inheritance to his children's children: and the wealth of the sinner is laid up for the just."
Proverbs 13:22

"The eyes of all wait upon thee; and thou givest them their meat in due season. Thou openest thine hand, and satisfiest the desire of every living thing."
Psalm 145:15 -16

"And they rose early in the morning, and went forth into the wilderness of Tekoa: and as they went forth, Jehoshaphat stood and said, Hear me, O Judah, and ye inhabitants of Jerusalem; Believe in the LORD your God, so shall ye be established; believe his prophets, so shall ye prosper."
2 Chronicles 20:20

"Let them shout for joy, and be glad, that favor my righteous cause: yea, let them say continually, Let the LORD be magnified, which hath pleasure in the prosperity of his servant." Psalm 35:27

"The LORD is my shepherd; I shall not want. He maketh me to lie down in green pastures: he leadeth me beside the still waters. He restoreth my soul: he leadeth me in the paths of righteousnessfor his name's sake.
Yea, though I walk through the valley of the shadow of death, I will fear no evil: for thou art with me; thy rod and thy staff they comfort me. Thou preparest a table before me in the presence of mine enemies: thou anointest my head with oil;
my cup runneth over. Surely goodness and mercy shall follow me all the days of my life: and I will dwell in the house of the LORD for ever."
Psalm 23:1-6

"Behold, God is mighty, and despiseth not any: he is mighty in strength and wisdom. He preserveth not the life of the wicked: but giveth right to the poor. He withdraweth not his eyes from the righteous: but with kings are they on the throne; yea, he doth establish them for ever, and they are exalted. And if they be bound in fetters, and be holden in cords of affliction; Then he sheweth them their work, and their transgressions that they have exceeded. He openeth also their ear to discipline, and commandeth that they return from iniquity. If they obey and serve him, they shall spend their days in prosperity, and their years in pleasures."
Job 36:5-11

"These have power to shut heaven, that it rain not in the days of their prophecy: and have power over waters to turn them to blood, and to smite the earth with all plagues, as often as they will."
Hebrews 11:6

*"Only be thou strong and very courageous, that thou mayest
observe to do according to all the law, which Moses my servant
commanded thee: turn not from it to the right hand or to the left,
that thou mayest prosper withersoever thou goest. This book of the law shall not depart
out of thy mouth; but thou shalt meditate therein day and night, that thou mayest
observe to do according to all that is written therein: for then thou shalt
make thy way prosperous, and then thou shalt have good success."*
Joshua 1:7-8

*"And keep the charge of the LORD thy God, to walk in his ways,
to keep his statutes, and his commandments, and his judgments,
and his testimonies, as it is written in the law of Moses, that thou
mayest prosper in all that thou doest, and whithersoever thou
turnest thyself:"*
1 Kings 2:3

"The thief cometh not, but for to steal, and to kill, and to destroy: I am come that they might have life, and that they might have it more abundantly."
John 10:10

"The righteous shall flourish like the palm tree: he shall grow like a cedar in Lebanon. Those that be planted in the house of the LORD shall flourish in the courts of our God. They shall still bring forth fruit in old age; they shall be fat and flourishing;"
Psalm 92:12-14

"The LORD will not suffer the soul of the righteous to famish: but he casteth away the substance of the wicked. He becometh poor that dealeth with a slack hand: but the hand of the diligent maketh rich."
Proverbs 10:3-4

"My son, let not them depart from thine eyes: keep sound wisdom and discretion: So shall they be life unto thy soul, and grace to thy neck. Then shalt thou walk in thy way safely, and thy foot shall not stumble. When thou liest down, thou shalt not be afraid: yea, thou shalt lie down, and thy sleep shall be sweet."
Proverbs 3:21-24

"In the house of the righteous is much treasure: but in the revenues of the wicked is trouble." *Proverbs 15:6*

"The soul of the sluggard desireth, and hath nothing: but the soul of the diligent shall be made fat." *Proverbs 13:4*

"Seest thou a man diligent in his business? he shall stand before kings; he shall not stand before mean men."
Proverbs 22:29

"He that tilleth his land shall have plenty of bread: but he that followeth after vain persons shall have poverty enough. A faithful man shall abound with blessings: but he that maketh haste to be rich shall not be innocent."
Proverbs 28:19-20

"If any of you lack wisdom, let him ask of God, that giveth to all men liberally, and upbraideth not; and it shall be given him. But let him ask in faith, nothing wavering. For he that wavereth is like a wave of the sea driven with the wind and tossed."
James 1:5-6

"Then shalt thou delight thyself in the LORD; and I will cause thee to ride upon the high places of the earth, and feed thee with the heritage of Jacob thy father: for the mouth of the LORD hath spoken it." Isaiah 58:14

*"But of him are ye in Christ Jesus, who of God is made unto us
wisdom, and righteousness, and sanctification, and redemption:"*
1 Corinthians 1:30

*"But thou shalt remember the LORD thy God: for it is he that
giveth thee power to get wealth, that he may establish his covenant which he sware
unto thy fathers, as it is this day. And it shall be, if thou do at all forget the LORD thy
God, and walk after other gods, and serve them, and worship them, I testify against
you this day that ye shall surely perish."*
Deuteronomy 8:18,19

*"For bodily exercise profiteth little: but godliness is profitable unto
all things, having promise of the life that now is, and of that which
is to come."*
1 Timothy 4:8

"The rich man's wealth is his strong city: the destruction of the poor is their poverty. The blessing of the LORD, it maketh rich, and he addeth no sorrow with it. The fear of the wicked, it shall come upon him: but the desire of the righteous shall be granted."
Proverbs 10:15,22,24

"If ye be willing and obedient, ye shall eat the good of the land:"   Isaiah 1:19

"Do not err, my beloved brethren. very good gift and every perfect gift is from above, and cometh down from the Father of lights, with whom is no variableness, neither shadow of turning."
James 1:16,17

"Keep therefore the words of this covenant, and do them, that ye may prosper in all that ye do."   Deuteronomy 29:9

*"And it shall come to pass, if thou shalt hearken diligently unto the
voice of the LORD thy God, to observe and to do all his commandments which I command thee this day, that the LORD thy God will set thee on high above
all nations of the earth: And all these blessings shall come on thee, and overtake thee,
if thou shalt hearken unto the voice of the LORD thy God. Blessed shalt
thou be in the city, and blessed shalt thou be in the field. Blessed shall be the fruit of
thy body, and the fruit of thy ground, and the fruit of thy cattle, the increase
of thy kine, and the flocks of thy sheep.
Blessed shall be thy basket and thy store.Blessed shalt thou be when thou comest in,
and blessed shalt thou be when thou goest out. The LORD shall cause thine enemies
that rise up against thee to be smitten before thy face: they shall come out against thee
one way, and flee before thee seven ways. The LORD shall command the
blessing upon thee in thy storehouses, and in all that thou settest thine hand unto; and
he shall bless thee in the land which the LORD thy God giveth thee.
Deuteronomy28:1-8*

The LORD shall establish thee an holy people unto himself, as he hath sworn unto thee, if thou shalt keep the commandments of the LORD thy God, and walk in his ways. And all people of the earth shall see that thou art called by the name of the LORD; and they shall be afraid of thee. And the LORD shall make thee plenteous in goods, in the fruit of thy body, and in the fruit of thy cattle, and in the fruit of thy ground, in the land which the LORD swear unto thy fathers to give thee.

The LORD shall open unto thee his good treasure, the heaven to give the rain unto thy land in his season, and to bless all the work of thine hand: and thou shalt lend unto many nations, and thou shalt not borrow. And the LORD shall make thee the head, and not the tail; and thou shalt be above only, and thou shalt not be beneath; if that thou hearken unto the commandments of the LORD thy God, which I command thee this day, to observe and to do them: And thou shalt not go aside from any of the words which I command thee this day, to the right hand, or to the left, to go after other gods to serve them."

Deuteronomy 28:9-14